The Story of Konkobre The Chick

By Somanegre Lydie K. Kafando   Illustrated by Sialoxy

To Lamoussa Theodore Kafando,

Dad, this is dedicated to you. I am honored to be your daughter. I always wanted to be like you, a loving, caring, and pleasant person to be around.

A Note From the Author

This story is the first story that I was able to remember as a child. I loved that whenever it was my turn to tell a story, it was always KonKobre. I was predictable that my sisters and cousins would chuckle. I decided to write it for my children. I initially wrote it in French in 2002 but never published it. This English version is to share the story with all children. I Kept the original illustrations to make it an activity book where children can color the illustrations.

Mom: "Tonight's story is my favorite."

KonKobre

It was the day before the great holiday of the Gallinaces. Everyone was getting ready for the holiday. The population gathered a variety of grains for the food, water, and decorations for their coops. Musicians were tuning their instruments; magicians were perfecting their tricks, and performers were fully rehearsing their lines, practicing their dance moves, and making their costumes.

There was joy in the atmosphere in the Gallimaces' village. All the birds were excited. Roosters, with big red combs, were cock-a-doodle-doing to wake everyone up. Turkeys were gobbling with enthusiasm. Male peacocks were strutting through the ground, showing off their beautifully designed patterns, and unfolding their long tails to exhibit a fan of ocellated feathers. Ash-grey partridges in the high weeds were screaming to make themselves heard. Dark feathered Guinea fowls with white dots were chasing each other to show themselves off. All the other birds were also getting ready for the great holiday.

In preparation for the next day, the female chicKens decided to go to the best beauty salon in the neighboring village. The salon was new. It had professional staff and the latest equipment. All the chicKens gathered outside the coop to begin their trip to the salon. KonKobre, a featherless chicK, decided to join the other chicKs, but as soon as she approached them, they started laughing when they saw her. The arrogant chicK, named Yare, pecKed her bacK and said: "KonKobre, in case you have forgotten, let me remind you that this gathering is for those with feathers. You should not bother to go to the salon. It is liKe looKing for lices on a bald head. Hahaha, what style can you possibly have? Go back to the coop to your poor mother so she can Keep you warm under her feathers in this cold weather." The other chicKs laughed at KonKobre and one mocKingly added: "Yeah, KonKobre! Go to the traditional healer and asK for an urgent fix for feathers by tomorrow."

Embarrassed but unbreakable, KonKobre, strong in character, proceeded to join the mean chicks quietly from a distance. During their journey, she walked as far as possible from the others, hearing them gossip and tease other chicks.

Suddenly, the clouds began to darKen, announcing a big storm. The chicks decided to find shelter to prevent their feathers from getting soaKed. They found an abandoned hut made of straws and rushed to shelter in it. While waiting for the rain to stop, they continued their conversation about the holiday, such as food, clothes, jewelry, and shoes. Some of them bragged about what their husband gave them for the celebration. The room was chattery, with conversation flowing among them except KonKobre, who was on her corner listening quietly and earnestly praying for the rain to stop.

Unfortunately, the joyful ambiance was cut short when the chicks heard a loud purring from the ceiling. The scary meowing caused a profound silence in the room. A big black cat with mirroring eyes jumped from the ceiling and landed at the entrance blocking the exit. The chicks were trapped and could not escape, so they became frozen in fear. The big black cat licked its lips happily, rubbed its paws to display them, and showed its pointy white teeth. He felt so confident and sure of his victory over his guests that he started singing proudly and loudly.

His lyrics made the chicks petrified. He continuously sang:

"Zii n zii m dogin
Ti Kom tar maam
Ti nemd wa pam maam
Id pus Wend barka."

"Sitting in my hut
Starving for fresh food
And meat came to me
Let's thank God!"

The big black cat's performance created fear among the chicks that they started to panic; some were shaking, others screaming for help, hoping to be heard and rescued by anyone. The anxiety was high among the chicks. They thought about how they would escape this starving black cat. The other chicks pushed KonKobre in front of the cat. She stood before the cat while he was still proudly performing.

At first, she was scared, but as she watched the cat perform, she recalled her mother's advice. She remembered words like, "Be brave, bold, kind, helpful, and clever." Unexpectedly, she started singing a tune with a lovely, piercing, and convincing voice.

"Tond da Kenga yadces weogo
tond da Kenga yadces weogo
Id Ku gnu raad a we
Gnu sablag Kang na ntoK piiga."

"We were in the Yadces
We were in the Yadces
We Killed nine cats
This blacK one will maKe it ten."

The confidence, braveness, and audacity of KonKobre, the featherless chicK, motivated the rest of the chicK to sing with her. As they sang together, they got louder and braver that they scared the big blacK cat, and it ran out of the hut. The chicKs felt relieved and happy that they were safe. The chicKs thanKed KonKobre for her braveness and for saving their lives. To thanK her, each chicK gave her a feather.

After the rain, the chicks continued their journey to the beauty salon. They all let KonKobre go first, and she had a beautiful style done to her feathers.

Back in the Gallinaces village, everyone heard the story of KonKobre being a hero. On the day of the holiday, she received honors from the village chief.

Lesson:

This story denotes that our differences should not define us, and we should not let other people humiliate or belittle us. Our uniqueness makes us specially designed for a purpose. We should turn the negative into positive.